THE CONSULTING WAY

ARVIND UPADHYAY

Think of this book as a sampler. You, the reader, need not start at the beginning and work your way through to the end. If you want to, feel free; otherwise, scan the table of contents and read whatever items interest you most.

Contents

CHAPTER ONE

WAY OF THINKING ABOUT BUSINESS PROBLEMS

The consultants who succeed love to solve problems.Problem solving isn't a thing you do ; it's what you do. It's almost as though you approached everything looking for ways it could be better, whatever it was. A part of you is always asking, "Why is something done this way? Is this the best way it can be done?" You have to be fundamentally skeptical about everything.

thinks about business problems. It shows what it means to be factbased, structured, and hypothesis-driven. It will tell you the way to approach a business problem, and offer you a few choice rules to live by when trying to solve them.

BUILDING THE SOLUTION

the Firm's problem-solving process has three major attributes. When team members meet for the first time to discuss their client's problem, they know that their solution will be

- Fact-based
- Rigidly structured
- Hypothesis-driven*

In this chapter, you will learn exactly what these attributes mean and how you can apply them in your business.

FACTS ARE FRIENDLY Facts are the bricks with which you will lay a path to your solution and build pillars to support it. Don't fear the facts. Problem solving at the Firm begins with facts. On the first day of an engagement, all members of the team comb through stacks of articles and internal research documents to gather enough facts to illuminate their piece of the problem for the first team meeting. Having drawn up an initial hypothesis for the problem, the team then races to gather the facts necessary (when put through the appropriate analyses) to support or refute it.

We dresses up its problem-solving process, it comes down to very careful, high-quality analysis of the components of the problem combined with an aggressive attitude toward fact gathering.

Why are facts so important to the consulting way does business? There are two reasons. First, facts compensate for lack of gut instinct (see " . . . But Every Client Is Unique" in Chapter 2). Most consultant-ites are generalists. They know a little about a lot of things. As they gain experience and move through the ranks, they may come to know a lot about a lot of things. Even at this point, however, they will still know less about, say, inventory.

management practices for perishable foodstuffs than the folks who have been running the distribution operations of Stop & Shop for the last 10 years. Gut instinct might tell those folks the solution to an inventory management problem in 10 seconds (although they still would be wise to check the facts); consulting way will go to the facts first.

Second, facts bridge the credibility gap. When she joins the Firm, the typical associate* (at least in the United States) will have graduated near the top of her college class, spent two or three years working for a large company, then received her MBA from a top business school. She will be in her mid- to late twenties. On her first engagement she may have to present her analysis to the CEO of a Fortune 50 company, who will not give much credence to what some newly minted, 27-year-old MBA has to say—unless she has an overwhelming weight of facts to back her up. This is just as true for a junior executive presenting a proposal to his boss. Despite (or possibly because of) the power of facts, many businesspeople fear them. Perhaps they are afraid that if they look too closely at the facts, they—or someone above them—might not like what they see. Maybe they think that if they don't look, the nasty facts will go away—but they won't. Hiding from the facts is a prescription for failure—eventually, truth will out. You must not fear the facts. Hunt for them, use them, but don't fear them.

To structure your thinking when solving business problems (or anything, for that matter), you must be complete while avoiding confusion and overlap.

MECE (pronounced "me-see") stands for "mutually exclusive, collectively exhaustive" and it is a sine qua non of the problem-solving process at The consulting way. MECE gets pounded into every new associate's head from the moment of entering the Firm. Every document (including internal memos), every presentation, every e-mail and voice mail produced by a The consulting way is supposed to be MECE. Ask any number of The consulting way what they remember most about the way the Firm solves problems and they will tell you, "MECE, MECE, MECE."

MECE structures your thinking with maximum clarity (hence minimum confusion) and maximum completeness. MECE starts at the top level of your solution—the list of issues making up the problem you have to solve. When you think you have determined the issues, take a hard look at them. Is each one a separate and distinct issue? If so, then your issue list is mutually exclusive. Does every aspect of the problem come under one (and only one) of these issues—that is, have you thought of everything? If so, then your issues are collectively exhaustive. Suppose your team is working on a study for that famous American manufacturing firm Acme Widgets. The problem you face is "We need to sell more widgets." Your team might come up with a list of the following ways to increase widget sales: • Changing the way we sell our widgets to retail outlets. • Improving the way we market our widgets to consumers. • Reducing the unit cost of our widgets.

f this list looks rather generic, that's fine; we will talk about moving down a level of detail in the next section. What matters is that the list is MECE. Suppose you add another item, say, "Reengineering our widget production process." How does that fit with the three issues you already have? This is certainly an important issue, but it isn't a fourth point alongside the others. It falls under "Reducing the unit cost," along with other subissues such as "Leveraging our distribution system" and "Improving our inventory management." Why? Because all these are ways to reduce the unit cost of widgets. Putting any (or all) of them with the other three issues on the list would cause an overlap. The items in the list would no longer be mutually exclusive. Overlap represents muddled thinking by the writer and leads to confusion for the reader. Once you have a list in which all the items are separate and distinct (i.e., mutually exclusive), you have to check that it also includes every issue or item relevant to the problem (i.e., it is collectively exhaustive). Go back for a moment to "Reengineering our widget production process." You put this under "Reducing the unit cost." Now one of your team members says, "We should think about ways to improve widget quality through the production process." She's right. Does this mean you should go back to having reengineering as an issue in its own right? No, but you should refine your list to include, under "Reducing unit cost," the subissue "Reengineering the production process to reduce unit cost," and, under "Improving the way we market . . . ," the subissue "Reengineering the production process to improve widget quality." Now you have something that looks like this: • Changing the way we sell our widgets to retail outlets. • Improving the way we market our widgets to consumers.

–Reengineering the production process to improve widget quality. • Reducing the unit cost of our widgets. –Reengineering the production process to reduce unit cost. Suppose your team has come up with some interesting ideas that don't fit under the main issues. What then? You could ignore those points, but that wouldn't help Acme. You could make them issues in their own right, but then you would have too many issues. A good consulting way issue list contains neither fewer than two nor more than five top-line issues (of course, three is best).

There is a solution to this dilemma—the magical category "Other Issues." If you can't figure out where to put those two or three brilliant ideas, there is always Other Issues. There is a caveat, however. Avoid using Other Issues in your top-line list—it looks out of place. It's fine lumped in among a bunch of subissues, but on the first slide of a big presentation, it sticks out. So try a little harder to fit those brilliant ideas into your top-line issues. Chances are you can. Still, if all else fails, Other Issues will help you stay MECE.

SOLVE THE PROBLEM AT THE FIRST MEETING—THE INITIAL HYPOTHESIS Solving a complex problem is like embarking on a long journey. The initial hypothesis is your problem-solving map.

The initial hypothesis (IH), the third pillar of the consulting way problem-solving process, is the most difficult to explain. To make the explanation easier for you (and me), I will break this section into three parts:

• Defining the initial hypothesis. • Generating the initial hypothesis. • Testing the initial hypothesis

The essence of the initial hypothesis is "Figure out the solution to the problem before you start." This seems counterintuitive, yet you do it all the time. Suppose you have to drive to a restaurant in a part of town you don't know. You know you have to make the third left off Smith Street and then take the first right; it's just after that corner. You know how to get to Smith Street; you'll just follow your directions from there. Congratulations, you have an initial hypothesis. Solving business problems is more complicated than finding a restaurant, but the initial hypothesis works the same way. It is a road map, albeit hastily sketched, to take you from problem to solution. If your IH is correct, then solving the problem means filling in the details of the map through factual analysis. Let's return to Acme Widgets from the last section. You and your team must find a way to increase sales at the widget business unit. After you've brainstormed using your knowledge of the widget business, but before you've spent a lot of time gathering and analyzing the facts, you might come up with the following top-line IH: We can increase widget sales by: • Changing the way we sell our widgets to retail outlets. • Improving the way we market our widgets to consumers. • Reducing the unit cost of our widgets. As I will show in the next section, you would then take each issue down to another level or two of detail to determine which analyses you need in order to prove or disprove each hypothesis. Remember that a hypothesis is merely a theory to be provedor disproved. It is not the answer. If your IH is correct, then, a few months down the road, it will be the first slide in your presentation. If it turns out to be wrong, then, by proving it wrong, you will have enough information to move toward the right answer. By putting your IH down on paper, and determining how you can prove or disprove it, you have set up a road map that you can follow to an eventual proved solution.

GENERATING THE INITIAL HYPOTHESIS

The IH emerges from the combination of facts and structure. Therefore, as the first step in generating an IH, you must start with the facts. Remember, however, that you don't want to do a lot of digging around for information before you know where to dig. One former consulting way SEM had a good approach for generating IHs:

At the start of an engagement, I would just try to digest as much of our fact base as possible. I would sit down with the trade publications in that industry for an hour or two—not so much to gather facts as to absorb something of the flavor of that industry: what the jargon is, what the current industry issues are. I would especially seek out people in the Firm who knew about this particular industry. That was the quickest, most efficient way to get up to speed. When generating an initial hypothesis, you don't need all the facts, just enough to have a good overview of the industry and the problem. If the problem is in your own business, you may already have the facts in your head. That's great, but facts are not enough. You have to apply structure to them. To structure your IH begin by breaking the problem into its components—the key drivers . Next, make an actionable recommendation regarding each driver. This is extremely important. Suppose your business's profits are greatly affected by the weather; in fact, it is the key determinant of profits in a given quarter. "We have to pray for good weather" is not an actionable recommendation. On the other hand, "We must reduce our vulnerability to changes in the weather" is an actionable, top-line recommendation. For your next step, you must take each top-line recommendation and break it down to the level of issues. If a given recommendation is correct, what issues does it raise? Consider the likely answers to each issue. Then go down another level. For each issue, what analyses would you need to make to prove or disprove your hypothesis? With a little experience, and a lot of debate within your team, you should get a good sense of what is provable and what is not. This will help you avoid blind alleys. In the Acme Widgets problem, suppose your team decided that the key drivers were the sales force, the consumer marketing strategy, and production costs. You then came up with a list of actionable, top-line recommendations as your initial hypothesis: We can increase widget sales by: • Changing the way we sell our widgets to retail outlets. • Improving the way we market our widgets to consumers. • Reducing the unit cost of our widgets.

Let's begin with a closer look at the sales force. It's organized geographically (Northeast, Mid-Atlantic, Southeast, etc.) and sells primarily to three types of retail outlets: superstores, department stores, and specialty stores. The team believes that the sales force ought to be organized by customer type—that's one issue. What analyses could prove or disprove that belief? You could break out the sales by customer type for each region. If penetration of superstores in the Northeast is higher than in any other region and higher than for the other types of retail outlets, find out why. When you talk to the Northeast sales reps, you might find that they have a better feel for superstores than any other sales team. What if they were put in charge of all superstores across the country and achieved the same penetration? What would that mean for widget sales? The end product of this exercise is what consultting way calls the issue tree. In other words, you start with your initial hypothesis and branch out at each issue. The result looks like the figure below. When you've completed your issue tree, you have your problem-solving map. That's the easy part. The difficult part will come when you have to dig deep to prove your hypothesis.

TESTING THE INITIAL HYPOTHESIS Before you take your problem-solving map out on the road, you want (forgive the mixed metaphor) to kick the tires on it. Test it. Is it the best possible hypothesis you could devise, given what you know about the industry and your client or company? Have you thought about all the issues? Have you considered all the drivers of the problem? Are all your recommendations actionable and provable? When I discussed generating an IH, I used the phrase "your team" rather than "you." My experience at consulting way taught me that IHs produced by teams are much stronger than those produced by individuals. Why? Most of us are poor critics of our own thinking. We need others to pick apart our ideas. A team of three or four bright individuals is an excellent vehicle for that. So when your team meets to come up with an IH let a thousand flowers bloom. Everyone should have his or her own ideas and initial hypotheses. Everyone should be prepared to push a teammate's thinking and test each new idea. If you are the team leader, you should try to be the thought leader too. Try to take a different approach from whatever has just been said. Ask, "What if we change this? What if we push that? How about looking at it this way?" The process involves shooting a certain amount of bull. That's OK, have fun—as long as it pushes your thinking.

CHAPTER TWO

DEVELOPING AN APPROACH

Just knowing the essence of the consulting way problem-solving process does not mean you can now go forth and conquer the business world by being fact-based, structured, and hypothesis-driven. No two business problems are identical; you must figure out how to approach each problem in order to devise the best solution for it. In this chapter, I will explain how the consulting way approach business problems and apply the consulting way problem-solving process to maximum effect.

THE PROBLEM IS NOT ALWAYS THE PROBLEM Sometimes a business problem will land on your desk and you will be told to solve it. Fair enough. But before you go rushing off in any particular direction, make sure you're solving the right problem—it may not be the one you were given.

A consulting way with a scientific background told me that business problem solving is organic and complex, like medicine. A patient will come into a doctor's office and say that he thinks he has the flu. He will tell the doctor about his symptoms: scratchy throat, achy head, and runny nose. The doctor will not immediately trust the patient's conclusion. She will take the patient's history, ask some probing questions, and then make her diagnosis. The patient may have the flu, or a cold, or something more serious, but the doctor will not rely on the patient to diagnose himself. At consulting way, we found that clients were often no better at diagnosing themselves than a doctor's patients. Sometimes, problems would come to us in extremely vague formulations. In my first study at the Firm, our team's mission was to help a New York investment bank "increase profitability"—the business equivalent of a patient telling the doctor "I don't feel well." In another case, a consulting way team went in to evaluate expansion opportunities for a division of a manufacturing company. After a few weeks of gathering and analyzing data, the team realized that what the division needed was not expansion; it was closure or sell-off. The only way to figure out if the problem you have been given is the real problem is to dig deeper. Get facts. Ask questions. Poke around. It usually does not take very long to figure out if you are heading down the right path, and the time you take up front will more than make up for itself in time you don't waste further down the line. What do you do when you are convinced you are working on the wrong problem? When a doctor thinks that a patient's minor symptoms mask something more serious, she will tell her patient, "Mr. Jones, I can treat your headache, but I think it's a symptom of something more serious and I'd like to do further tests." In the same way, you should go back to your client, or your boss—whoever it was that asked for your input in the first place—and say, "You asked me to look at problem X, but the real impact on our performance will come from solving problem Y. Now I can solve problem X, if that's what you really want, but I think it's in our interest to focus on Y." If you have the data to back you up, the client can either accept your recommendation or tell you to stay on the original problem, but you will have fulfilled your responsibility to act in the client's best interests.

Most business problems resemble each other more than they differ. This means that with a small number of problem-solving techniques, you can answer a broad range of questions. These techniques may be somewhere in your organization, either written down or in the heads of your fellow employees. If not, use your experience to develop your own tool kit. Pandit & company , like every other consulting firm, has developed a number of problem-solving methods and given them fancy names: Analysis of Value Added, Business Process Redesign, Product-Market Scan, and so on. These techniques are immensely powerful. They allow consultants very rapidly to fit the raw data that lands on their desks into a coherent framework and give them insights into the nature of the client's problem. The consultants can then focus their thinking on the "drivers" of the problem and start working toward a solution.

We The consulting way made frequent use of an analytical framework called Forces at Work. It proved especially valuable at the start of an engagement in helping us look at the likely external pressures on the client. The technique involves identifying the client's suppliers, customers, competitors, and possible substitute products. We then list all the changes occurring in each of the four categories. What impact— positive or negative—could these have on our client? Also, what internal changes are affecting the client and the client's industry? Which of these factors could actually cause major changes to the way the client designs, manufactures, distributes, sells, and services its products? Whatever business you're in, this framework will not only help you build a snapshot of your competitive environment, but also help you develop a view of how that environment might change. Try it. It sounds simple, but it is a powerful way to stimulate your thinking about strategic business problems. These frameworks really help at the start of the problem-solving process. For instance, when I was a second-year associate, I joined a team that was helping a major Wall Street investment bank reorganize its information technology department. All the executives at the bank wanted IT reorganized, but not if it meant any changes in the way their computers were supported. The IT department was a real mess, with 600 employees, a dozen different subdepartments, and a web of reporting relationships that made my head spin.

That there are many similarities between business problems does not mean that similar problems have similar solutions. You have to validate your initial hypothesis (or your gut) with fact-based analysis. This will put you in a much better position to get your ideas accepted.

If all you have is a hammer, then every problem looks like a nail. Critics of consulting way (and management consulting in general) say that the Firm bases its solutions on the most current management fad—the favorite tool in its intellectual toolbox. At the Firm, at least, this is untrue. Fact-based analysis as practiced by consulting way requires hard proof before any recommendations are made to clients. THE CONSULTING WAY , puts it like this: People think that the Firm—and management consultants in general—have a precanned answer. That is certainly not the case at CONSULTING ; if it were, then the CONSULTING WAY would not be as successful as it is.

The tools may be the same from problem to problem, but you have to apply them. For instance, in my experience, in 8 out of 10 pricing problems the answer turns out to be "raise your prices." If you do the fact-based analysis— demand curves, breakeven calculations, budgets—enough times, you see almost invariably that firms should be raising their prices. But if you automatically say that's the answer, you'll get into trouble, because you'll run into an instance where the answer is really "lower your prices." As a corollary to avoiding cookie-cutter solutions, be careful about blindly trusting your gut. As you gain experience in business, as you see and solve more and more problems, you will get a fair idea of what works in your industry and what doesn't. Although your gut will often be right, take a hint from former President Reagan: "Trust and verify."

MAKE SURE YOUR SOLUTION FITS YOUR CLIENT The most brilliant solution, backed up by libraries of data and promising billions in extra profits, is useless if your client or business can't implement it. Know your client. Know the organization's strengths, weaknesses, and capabilities—what management can and cannot do. Tailor your solutions with these factors in mind.

THE CONSULTING WAY -

We were doing a cost cutting study for a large financial institution. We discovered that they were in the midst of linking all their offices—they had several hundred around the world—by satellite. This project had begun several years previously, and they had managed so far to roll it out to about half their offices. We determined that with currently available technology they could do the same thing for a fraction of the cost using conventional phone lines. By our calculations, they would have saved $170 million on a present value basis. We took our findings to the senior manager overseeing the engagement, the man who had brought us in to begin with, and he said, "Well, that's terrific. We appreciate that it could have saved us a few hundred million dollars, but we've already started down this road and, politically, it's just too risky. You have to realize that we only have a certain amount of energy in the organization and, frankly, we need ideas that are bigger than this." At one level, it's unbelievable that he didn't accept our idea. But on another level, we were coming up with other suggestions that would save the organization half a billion or a billion dollars. So this was, if not exactly chicken feed, just a medium-size payoff for them. It's a rational response. If I can do only three things, I'll do the three biggest.

Unfortunately, when academic ideals meet business realities, business realities usually win. Businesses are full of real people, with real strengths and weaknesses and limitations. These people can do only so much with the finite resources available in their organizations. Some things they just cannot do, whether for political reasons, lack of resources or inability.

As a consultant, you bear the responsibility for knowing the limitations of your client; if your client is your own employer—or your own business—that responsibility is doubled. Knowing those limitations, you must make sure that any recommendations you make fit within them.

SOMETIMES YOU HAVE TO LET THE SOLUTION COME TO YOU The CONSULTING WAY rules of problem solving, like all rules, have their exceptions. You will not be able to form an initial hypothesis every time. Sometimes, the client will not know what the problem is, just that there is a problem. Other times, the scope of your project will be so large—or so vague—that starting with an IH will be worthless. Still other times, you will be breaking new ground and nothing in your experience will point to a solution. Don't panic! If you get your facts together and do your analyses, the solution will come to you.

SOME PROBLEMS YOU JUST CAN'T SOLVE . . . SOLVE THEM ANYWAY Eventually, you will run into a brick wall that is tougher than your head. Don't keep pounding; it has no effect on the wall and does your head no good.

Redefine the problem. You can tell your client that the problem is not X, it's Y. This is especially useful when you know that solving Y will add a lot of value, where as trying to wrestle with X would cost a lot of time and resources for little result. If you make this switch very early on, you show great business judgment; if you do it after several weeks" work, you risk being accused of a cop out.

Tweak your way to a solution. Sometimes you will come up with a great solution that you know the client organization cannot implement. This is especially true with organizational change—it is easy to devise an optimal organization, but you usually have to deal with the personnel resources that the client already has. When that happens to you, expand your time horizon. Don't worry about implementing your solution immediately. As people leave the organization, you can "tweak" your way to your optimum over time. Work through the politics. Even political problems are soluble. Most people in business are rational, at least in their business conduct. They react to incentives. Therefore, when you face political opposition, it usually means that your solution has negative implications for someone in the organization. So politics is just people acting in their own interests. To work through the politics, you must think about how your solution affects the players in an organization. You must then build a consensus for change that takes account of the different incentives and organizational factors driving the politics. Consensus building may require you to change your solution to make it acceptable. Do it. Remember that politics is the art of the possible, and it's no good devising the ideal solution if the client refuses to accept it.

CHAPTER THREE

80/20 AND OTHER RULES

This chapter contains a number of rules that consulting way consultants have found useful when trying to solve problems. They are difficult to classify. Call them my "Other Issues."

The 80/20 rule is one of the great truths of management consulting and, by extension, of business. You will see it wherever you look: 80 percent of your sales will come from 20 percent of your sales force; 20 percent of a secretary's job will take up 80 percent of her time; 20 percent of the population controls 80 percent of the wealth. It doesn't always work (sometimes the bread falls butter-side up), but if you keep your eyes peeled for examples of 80/20 in your business, you will come up with ways to improve it

I saw the 80/20 rule at work all the time at McKinsey, and I've always been impressed by its power as a problem-solving rule of thumb.

In my first-ever consulting way study, when I was between years at business school, I joined a team working with a large New York brokerage house. The board of directors wanted consulting way to show them how to improve the profitability of their institutional equity brokerage business—the selling of stocks to large pension funds and mutual funds like Fidelity and T. Rowe Price. When a client asks the question "How do I boost my profits?" the first thing The consulting way does is take a step back and ask the question "Where do your profits come from?" The answer to this is not always obvious, even to people who have been in their particular business for years. To answer this question for our client, our team went through every account of every broker and every trader by customer. We spent several weeks analyzing this mountain of data from every conceivable angle, but when we ran the numbers there are some of the first things we saw:

• 80 percent of the sales came from 20 percent of the brokers. • 80 percent of the orders came from 20 percent of the customers. • 80 percent of the trading profit came from 20 percent of the traders. These results pointed to some serious problems in the way the client allocated its staff resources, and we focused on those like a laser. Once we started digging, we found that the situation was more complex than simply "80 percent of the sales staff is lazy or incompetent" (not that we ever thought that was the case to begin with). We discovered, to give one example, that our client's three top brokers handled the 10 biggest accounts. By sharing these big accounts out among more brokers, and by dedicating one senior and one junior broker to each of the three largest customers, we actually increased total sales from these accounts. Rather than divide up the pie more fairly, we increased the size of the pie. Thus, 80/20 gave us a jump-start in solving the client's problem. 80/20 is all about data. What are your sales figures by product? What is your margin by product? How does each member of your sales team perform in terms of sales? In terms of profits? What is the success rate of your research teams? What is the geographical distribution of your customers? If you know your business well (and you'd better if you want to survive), then you know the right questions to ask. When you have your data, put it on a spreadsheet or in a database. Sort it in various ways. Play with the numbers. You will begin to see patterns, clumps that stand out. Those patterns will highlight aspects of your business that you probably did not realize. They may mean problems (a big problem if 80 percent of your profits come from 20 percent of your product lines), but they also mean opportunities. Find the opportunities and make the most of them.

DON'T BOIL THE OCEAN Work smarter, not harder. There's a lot of data out there relating to your problem, and a lot of analyses you could do. Ignore most of them.

The Consulting Way gathers enough facts to prove or disprove a hypothesis or support or refute an analysis—and only enough facts. This is the flip side of fact-based analysis in a business situation. Anything more is a waste of time and effort when both are precious commodities. I had this lesson brought home to me late one night while I was drafting a "fact pack" on a client's competitor. I had gathered a mountain of data and was trying to wring out a few new insights from it. My EM, Vik, walked into my office, briefcase and coat in hand, and asked how my work was going. I told him it was going well, but I thought I could pull together a few more charts. He picked up my draft, leafed through it, and said, "Ethan, it's eleven o'clock.

The client will love this. No one will be able to absorb more than you have here. Call it a day. Don't boil the ocean." We shared a cab home. "Don't boil the ocean" means don't try to analyze everything. Be selective; figure out the priorities of what you are doing. Know when you have done enough, then stop. Otherwise, you will spend a lot of time and effort for very little return, like boiling the ocean to get a handful of salt.

FIND THE KEY DRIVERS Many factors affect your business. Focus on the most important ones—the key drivers

In any consulting way team meeting where problem solving is on the agenda, someone will use the inelegant phrase "key drivers," as in, "Vik, I think these are the key drivers of this issue." In other words, there may be a 100 different factors affecting the sales of our widgets—weather, consumer confidence, raw material prices— but the three most important ones are X, Y, and Z. We'll ignore the rest. Engineers learn something called the Square Law of Computation. It states that for every component of a system—for every additional equation in a problem—the amount of computation required to solve the system increases at least as fast as the square of the number of equations. In other words, if the complexity of your problem doubles, the time it takes to solve it quadruples— unless you make some simplifications. For example, our solar system contains millions of objects, all having gravitational effects on one another. When analyzing planetary motion, astronomers start by ignoring most of these objects.* Focusing on the key drivers means drilling down to the core of the problem, rather than picking the whole problem apart piece by piece, layer by layer. Then, you can apply thorough, fact-based analysis where it will do the most good and avoid going down blind alleys.

Syntactical foibles aside, "key drivers" is a very powerful concept. It saves you time. It saves you effort. It keeps you from boiling the ocean. THE ELEVATOR TEST Know your solution (or your product or business) so thoroughly that you can explain it clearly and precisely to your client (or customer or investor) in 30 seconds. If you can do that, then you understand what you're doing well enough to sell your solution. Imagine it's time for that big, end-of-engagement presentation. You and your team have been up until 2 a.m. putting together your blue books,* making sure that every i has been dotted and every t crossed. You're all wearing your best suits and trying to look on the ball. The senior executives of your Fortune 50 client, anxious to hear consulting ways's words of wisdom, are taking their places around the boardroom table on the top floor of the corporate skyscraper. The CEO strides into the room and says, "Sorry, folks. I can't stay. We have a crisis and I have to go meet with our lawyers." Then he turns to you and says, "Why don't you ride down in the elevator with me and tell me what you've found out?" The ride will take about 30 seconds. In that time, can you tell the CEO your solution? Can you sell him your solution? That's the elevator test. Many companies use the elevator test (or something similar) because it's an excellent way of making sure that their executives'

time gets used efficiently. Procter & Gamble tells its managers to write one-page memos. A Hollywood producer will tell a screenwriter to "give me the bullet" on a new script; if, after 30 seconds, the producer likes what she's heard, the writer will get a chance to talk further, and maybe make a sale. Jason Klein instituted the elevator test when he took over as president of Field & Stream: My sales force could not explain the magazine to customers. Our advertisement space was shrinking. Then I trained my entire sales force on the elevator test. I challenged them to explain the magazine to me in 30 seconds. It became a valuable tool for them, and our ad base has grown every year. How do you encapsulate six months' work in 30 seconds? Start with the issues that your team addressed. The client wants to know the recommendations for each issue and the payoff. If you have a lot of recommendations, stick to the three most important—the ones with the biggest payoffs. Don't worry about the supporting data; you can talk about that when you have more time. For example, your analysis shows that a manufacturing client can't sell enough widgets because its sales force is organized by territory when it should be organized by buyer category. You have lots of data illustrating this: analyses of salespeople by buyer type, buyer interviews, field visits to retail and wholesale outlets, and so forth. When you're on that elevator ride, just tell the CEO, "We think you can boost sales of widgets by 50 percent in three years if you reorganize your sales force by buyer category. We can talk about the details later. Good luck with the lawyers."

PLUCK THE LOW-HANGING FRUIT Sometimes in the middle of the problem-solving process, opportunities arise to get an easy win, to make immediate improvements, even before the overall problem has been solved. Seize those opportunities! They create little victories for you and your team. They boost morale and give you added credibility by showing anybody who may be watching that you're on the ball and mean business.

At my stockbroker client, after we had derived a number of insights (thanks to 80/20) from our analysis of sales and trading data, we wanted to communicate our findings to the senior managers of the institutional equities department. We set up a meeting with the department head and the heads of all the business units in the division: sales, trading, research, and so on. Since I had taken the lead in the actual analysis of the data, I got to present our findings. They hit this group of very experienced Wall Street executives like a hammer. The client had no idea just how inefficient its operation was. The presentation had two important effects. First, it convinced those executives who had not been particularly keen on consulting way's presence in the first place that they had a problem and we could help solve it. Second, because I had presented the findings, their opinion of me rose quite sharply and my job became a lot easier. Before the meeting, I was some smart-ass MBA poking around their business. After the meeting, I was someone who was working for them to solve their problems. By plucking the low-hanging fruit, by resisting the temptation to hoard our information until some big end-of-study presentation, we made our client more enthusiastic, our jobs easier, and ourselves happier.

This rule is really about satisfying your customer in a longterm relationship. Your customer could be the purchaser of your products, or it could be a client for your services, or it could be your boss. Whoever it is, it pays to keep him happy and let him know that he is your top priority. If you are on, say, a software design project with a three-month lead time and you've put together a usable program that solves part of the problem in two weeks, show it to your boss. Don't wait! Solving only part of a problem can still mean increased profits. Just don't let anybody think you've given up on a complete solution. Those little wins help you and your customers.

MAKE A CHART EVERY DAY During the problem-solving process, you learn something new every day. Put it down on paper. It will help you push your thinking. You may use it, or you may not, but once you have crystalized it on the page, you won't forget it. Making a chart every day may strike you as somewhat anal-retentive. It is. Then again, when you are trying to craft facts into solutions, that is not so bad.

In the course of a typical day at counsulting way, you could start with a quick brainstorming session at 9 a.m., move on to a client interview at 10, a factory tour at 11, and then a sandwich lunch with your director. You might follow this with more client interviews, an end-of-day team meeting, and then a quick trip down to Wharton to participate in a recruiting seminar. In the midst of all this, it is very easy for the facts to blend into one another like pools of different-colored inks on a sheet of blotting paper. Even if you take good notes at your interviews and have the minutes of your team meetings, important points could get lost.

You can avoid this by sitting down for half an hour at the end of the day and asking yourself, "What are the three most important things I learned today?" Put them down in a chart or two— nothing fancy; neatness doesn't count. If the facts don't lend themselves to charting just write them down as bullet points. Put your results someplace where they won't get lost—don't just toss them into your in-tray. Later, when you are in analysis mode, you can come back to your charts and notes and think about what they mean and where they fit in terms of your solution. Of course, this little tip can be taken too far. One EM from Germany, while working out of the New York office, would write a whole presentation every night. I wouldn't recommend this for most people—at least those with a life. Then again, the EM was far from home, didn't know anyone in town, and had nothing better to do. He should have followed some of the suggestions presented in Part Four.

HIT SINGLES You can't do everything, so don't try. Just do what you're supposed to do and get it right. It's much better to get to first base consistently than to try to hit a home run—and strike out 9 times out of 10.

It took several years of gaining perspective before I understood the wisdom of the CEO's words. There are three reasons he was right: • It's impossible to do everything yourself all the time. • If you manage it once, you raise unrealistic expectations from those around you. • Once you fail to meet expectations, it is very difficult to regain credibility.

It's impossible to do everything yourself all the time. Business problems are complicated—the problems THE CONSULTING WAY deals with especially so. If you don't leverage the other members of your team to solve these problems, you are wasting valuable resources. The principle applies as much to senior managers as to junior executives whose MBA diplomas are still wet with ink. Very few people have the brainpower and energy to be a one-man show all the time.

If you manage it once, you raise unrealistic expectations from those around you. Suppose, for a moment, that you manage, through superhuman effort, to perform well beyond what is normally expected of you. You hit that ball out of the park and (what the heck) the bases were loaded. Congratulations. Of course, now your boss or your shareholders will expect you to do the same thing every time you step up to the plate. Once you fail to meet expectations, it is very difficult to regain credibility. Consulting way, it is said that you are only as good as your last study. If you have one "bad" engagement, all your hard work before that doesn't matter. EMs won't want you on their teams. You won't be staffed on the interesting projects. You won't be put in a position to excel.

The same thing happens in the stock market. A high-flying company that posts 20 percent profit increases every year sees its stock price soar. When it misses one quarter, even by as little as a cent, its momentum reverses. Wall Street drops the stock like a hot potato and its share price plummets. After that, even when the company gets back on the growth track, several years can go by before investors trust it enough to pile back in. When I was a kid, I had a fantasy baseball board game. You picked your team from a combination of then current players (Carl Yastrzemski, Sandy Koufax, Roberto Clemente) and baseball legends (Ruth, Cobb, DiMaggio). Each player came on a circle of paper marked out in sections printed with a result: single, double, home run, strikeout, and so forth. The size of each section depended on the player's career record. To play the game, you'd put the circle around a little pointer and spin the pointer; wherever it landed was the result for that player's turn at bat. The one thing I remember from that game was that the home run kings like Ruth, DiMaggio, and Aaron had the biggest strikeout zones too. It's all very well to talk of the necessity to strive purposefully and, if you fail, to fail gloriously. It's OK for Mark McGwire to strike out a lot, as long as he keeps hitting those home runs. In the business world, though, you're much better off hitting singles.

LOOK AT THE BIG PICTURE Every now and then, take a mental step back from whatever you're doing. Ask yourself some basic questions: How does what you're doing solve the problem? How does it advance your thinking? Is it the most important thing you could be doing right now? If it's not helping, why are you doing it? When you are trying to solve a difficult problem for your client or company, you can easily lose sight of your goal amid the million and one demands on your time. It's like you are hip-deep in a bog, following a muddy channel that you can't see. Analysis B follows analysis A and seems in turn to be followed seamlessly by analysis C. New data comes in and points to yet more analyses with which to fill your days (and nights). When you're feeling swamped by it all, take a metaphorical step back and figure out what it is you're trying to achieve. Do this by looking at "the big picture": the set of issues that make up your operating hypothesis. How does what you're doing fit into the big picture? A particular analysis may be intellectually correct, even interesting, but if it doesn't take you closer to a solution, it's a waste of time. Figure out your priorities; you can do only so much in a day. There is nothing quite so frustrating as looking back over the course of a day or week and realizing, not that you haven't come up with any end products, but that what you have come up with is worthless in terms of the problem at hand.

JUST SAY, "I DON'T KNOW" The Firm pounds the concept of professional integrity into its associates from their first day on the job, and rightly so. One important aspect of professional integrity is honesty—with your clients, your team members, and yourself. Honesty includes recognizing when you haven't got a clue. Admitting that is a lot less costly than bluffing. It was the morning of an important progress meeting at our client, a Fortune 50 manufacturing company. The team and John, our ED,* were going over the various sections of the presentation. I had already been through my piece of it; I had been up until 4 a.m. getting it ready and I was exhausted. As the discussion moved to another section, one that I had nothing to do with and knew little about, my brain started slipping into that blissful place known as sleep. I could hear the other members of the team discussing various points, but their words slipped away from my mind like water through a child's cupped fingers. Suddenly, my reverie evaporated as John asked me, "So, Ethan, what do you think about Suzie's point?" Momentary shock and fear yielded to concentration as I tried to recall what had just been said. Years of Ivy League and business school reflexes took over and I came out with a few lines of general agreement. Of course, what I said might just as well have come out of a horse's backside. If I had told John, "I'm not really sure—I haven't looked at this issue before," I would have been fine. Even if I had said, "Sorry, I just lost it for a minute," he would have understood; after all, he had been through exactly the same experience, like every other consulting way. Instead, I tried to fake it, and ended up slipping in my own horsefeathers. At the end of the engagement, several weeks later, the team had its final party. We went out to TGI Friday's, ate a lot of nachos, and drank a lot of beer. Then the EM began presenting each of the team members with presents of a rude and/or humorous nature.

DON'T ACCEPT "I HAVE NO IDEA" People always have an idea if you probe just a bit. Ask a few pointed questions—you'll be amazed at what they know. Combine that with some educated guessing, and you can be well along the road to the solution. If you ask people a question about their business and they tell you, "I have no idea," don't just walk away in defeat. "I have no idea" is a code; it really means, "I'm too busy to take the time to think about this," or "I don't think I'm smart enough to know about these things," or worst of all "I'm too lazy to come up with anything useful." Don't accept "I have no idea"—treat it as a challenge. Like the sculptor who turned a block of marble into an elephant by chiseling away everything that didn't look like an elephant, you must chip away at "I have no idea" with pointed questions. When Jason Klein wanted to put together a new business unit, he was sure that his top competitor was outspending him by a factor of 10. How could he prove this to his board of directors so they would give him more funding? He told his team to put together a P&L (profit and loss statement) for the competitor that showed what it was spending. As he recalls it: When I first suggested that we do this analysis, my people said, "We have no idea." So I challenged them. Did they know how much our competitor was spending on advertising? No, but they could make an educated guess. Did they know how much our competitor was spending on production costs? No, but they could make an estimate of the competitor's cost per issue and multiply that by reported circulation. And so it went. In the end, we put together a pretty comprehensive P&L backed up by solid assumptions. It may have been off by a factor of 2, but who cares? What mattered was that it was accurate enough to make the business decision that was on the table. Just as you shouldn't accept "I have no idea" from others, so you shouldn't accept it from yourself, or expect others to accept it from you. This is the flip side of "I don't know." With a bit of thinking and searching, you will usually find that you do know or can find out something about a question or issue (unless, of course, you have fallen asleep in the middle of a team meeting).

CHAPTER FOUR

ABOUT THE SELLING PROCESS THE CONSULTING WAY

The selling process at THE CONSULTING WAY differs from that of most organizations because, as any THE CONSULTING WAY will tell you, the Firm doesn't sell. The Firm may not sell, but it certainly brings in a continuing and growing volume of business, so there's something to be learned from the way THE CONSULTING WAY gets itself through its clients' doors. Getting your foot through the door is only half the battle when marketing your skills as a problem solver, however. You also have to put together your problem-solving package in way that ensures your success. THE CONSULTING WAY has learned a thing or two about that as well. In this chapter, we will look at the salesmanship and learn how to trim a problem-solving project to a manageable size and scope.

HOW TO SELL WITHOUT SELLING Business problems are like mice. They go unnoticed until they start nibbling your cheese. Just building a better mousetrap will not make the world beat a path to your door. People who don't have mice won't be interested—until the mice show up; then they need to know you have the mousetrap. This might sound like the musings of a Zen monk (or perhaps a management consultant from California). But sometimes the right way to sell your product or service is not to barge into your customer's home with a bunch of free samples. Just be there, at the right time, and make sure the right people know who you are.

Maintains a vast network of informal contacts with potential clients as well. The Firm encourages its partners to participate in "extracurricular activities" such as sitting on the boards of charities, museums, and cultural organizations; many members of these boards are executives at current or potential clients. consultants also address industry conferences.

Occasional meetings with former clients allow partners not only to check up on the effects of past projects, but to make sure that the Firm maintains some "share of mind" should new problems arise at the client.

These efforts could not be construed as selling, but they make sure that the right people know the Firm is there. That keeps the phones ringing. If you're in sales, then you probably do have to make the cold calls. For some people that is the fun of selling. But even the best foot-in-the-door saleswoman needs to market. You may not be on the same charitable board as billionaire investor Warren Buffett, but you can still find ways to network with existing and potential clients and customers. Trade shows, and conferences, even the right bars, will give you the chance to make sure they know who you are. Does your particular field have a trade journal? These magazines are always looking for copy from industry insiders: Write a good article and you will get your name in front of people who would otherwise never have heard of you. Meet your competitors too. Today's competitor could change jobs and become tomorrow's customer. Make sure he knows you! It all adds up to making sure your name is the one your customers think of when they have a need you can fill.

BE CAREFUL WHAT YOU PROMISE: STRUCTURING AN ENGAGEMENT When structuring your project, whether you are selling your services as a consultant or have been picked by your organization to solve an internal problem, don't bite off more than you can chew. Set definite milestones that you can meet. That way, you'll have targets you can achieve and your client will be satisfied.

When clients come with a problem, they want it fixed yesterday and for nothing. Fortunately, most clients realize that this desire is just slightly unrealistic. Still, when structuring an engagement, (usually in the person of a DCS* or ED) faces a lot of pressure to deliver the maximum results in the minimum time. THE CONSULTING WAY bills by the hour, and those hours do not come cheap.

The ED (or whoever is structuring the engagement) stands between the client and its demands on one side, and the engagement team on the other. The team can be pushed only so far for so long before the quality of its work begins to decline. consultants, in general, work very hard over the course of a study, but they do have limits; they also have lives, which they would like, at least occasionally, to live. The challenge for the ED is to balance the desires and budget constraints of the client with the limits of the team. The ideal synthesis of these two opposing forces is a project that a team of four to six consultants can complete in three to six months and that will produce tangible results for the client.

As the Firm spends time within a client organization, it almost always uncovers new problems that could benefit from expertise. These problems, however must be addressed at another time and in another engagement. Consequently, engagements tend to generate new business of their own accord. Thus, as long as the client is happy with the results that the Firm produces, THE CONSULTING WAY is likely to have a stream of new business (for which it often will not need to compete). As an organization, CONSULTING WAY extremely good at figuring out how much a team can do over the length of a typical study. The best EDs can balance the competing demands of client and team to a nicety; they tell the client, "We're going to do X and Y. We could do Z, but it would kill the team," while telling the team, "Look, we've already promised the client that we would do Z, so we've got to deliver." They then work the team to its limit while simultaneously making the client feel that he is getting value for money and exceeding his expectations. Of course, not every ED is that good. In my time at the Firm, certain EDs had reputations for overpromising to the client and then putting their teams through hell. They were to be avoided, along with EDs who were vague about the exact nature of the end product of a study and left the team to figure out just what it was supposed to do. What lessons does the experience give for the way you should structure your problem-solving project? If you are a consultant putting together a proposal for an outside client, then the answer is simple: Don't bite off more than you (and your team) can chew and know what your end product is going to be. If your boss steps into your office and says, "We have a little problem and we want you to head up a team to solve it," then the lesson for you is a bit more complicated. Don't blithely accept the assignment and say, "Sure, boss." If you do, you could be setting yourself up for a fall. Before you go hot footing it in search of a solution, get a feel for the scope of the problem. Is it something you and your team can solve in the time allotted? If not, either get more time or, even better, sit down with your boss and break the problem down into bite-size chunks. Figure out what the end product of each chunk will be: a recommendation, an implementation plan, a new product design, and so forth. Figure out what resources you will need to reach your goal and get a commitment from your boss that you will have them. Doing all this ahead of time can save you a lot of grief a few months down the road. Structuring your project properly at the beginning may not guarantee your success, but it at least gets you off to the right start.

CHAPTER FIVE

ASSEMBLING A TEAM

At consulting way, you never walk alone—or, at least, you never work alone. Everything at the Firm happens in teams, from front-line work on client engagements all the way up to firmwide decision making. The smallest team I ever worked on consisted of me and my EM on a pro bono engagement for a New York theater company. At the other end of the scale, the Firm's largest clients might have several five- or six-person teams working on site at one time; together, these form a "metateam." In the early 1990s, members of the AT&T metateam decided to get together to discuss their work; the Firm's headquarters didn't have a room large enough to hold them all, so they had to book a New Jersey hotel. consulting way relies on teams because they are the best way to solve the problems that the Firm's clients face. The complexity of these problems makes it impossible for one person to solve them—at least to the Firm's high standards. More people mean more hands to gather and analyze data and, more important, more minds to figure out what the data really mean. If you face complex problems in your business, you should probably put together a team to help solve them too. In the face of complexity, many hands don't just make light work; they make for a better result.

The Firm has developed a number of strategies for putting together and maintaining high-performance teams. In this chapter, you will learn how to select the right people for your team. You will also discover some tricks for keeping your team happy and productive under pressure.

GETTING THE MIX RIGHT You can't just throw four random people at a problem and expect them to solve it. Think about what sorts of skills and personalities will work best for your project. Then choose your teammates carefully.

To succeed as a business problem solver, you must choose your team carefully, getting the best mix of people from the resources you have available. consulting benefits from a global pool of talented, intelligent individuals whose strengths and weaknesses the Firm tracks closely. Even with this advantage, EMs and EDs must learn the art of team selection. Their experiences can help you, even if you can't call on the same level of resources. consulting way subscribe to one of two theories of team selection. The first theory states that intellectual horsepower is everything—find the smartest people for your team regardless of their experience or personal hygiene. The second theory says that what really matters is specific experience and skills; intelligence is a given within the Firm—every consultant is smart or he wouldn't be there. Neither of these theories is completely correct, but neither of them is completely wrong either. Proper team selection varies from problem to problem and client to client. Some problems will yield only to large amounts of analytical firepower. For instance, if you have mountains of complex data that you need to decipher, then you want the two or three best number crunchers that you can find, regardless of whether they can simultaneously walk and chew gum. On the other hand, if you are managing a big reorganization during which many sensitive decisions will have to be made, you would prefer to have someone on your team with good people skills and experience in implementing change. Another important team selection lesson emerges from the consulting team assignment process. When an engagement begins, the EM and ED pick their associates from the pool of available resources at the time. The "manager of associate development" or the office manager will tell them who is available and give them a sheet listing each associate's experience and rating each one on analytical ability, client management skills, and so forth. The biggest mistake in team selection comes from taking those ratings at face value. A smart EM always talks to potential team members before taking them on. By extension, if you are in a position to pick your team members before embarking on a project, never just accept people who are supposed to be good. Meet them face to face. Talk to them; see what's behind the recommendations. Maybe in her last assignment Sally just got lucky. Or maybe Pete's the CEO's nephew and his last boss was scared to tell the truth about him. (Of course, if he is the CEO's nephew, you may be stuck with him.) Maybe Carol's brilliant, but after spending 15 minutes talking to her, you know she would drive you crazy if she were on your team. Just remember, if you are lucky enough to be able to choose whom you will work with, choose wisely.

A LITTLE TEAM BONDING GOES A LONG WAY It's a truism that a team will perform better and its members will have a better time if the team members get along well. As a team leader, you should make an effort to promote team bonding; just make sure it doesn't become a chore.

team-bonding activities are a given. In the course of an engagement, you expect to go out at least a few times to the nicest restaurants in town, or to see a show or a game on consulting way (and, eventually, the client's) nickel. One ED even took his whole team to Florida for a long weekend. As a team leader, the question for you is how much formal team bonding is enough. After talking with a number of former consultants, and reflecting on my own experience, I'm going to go out on a limb and say that the answer is not much. A little team bonding goes a long way. As a team leader, you have the far more important job of looking after team morale (see the next section). Former SEM Abe Bleiberg put it like this: I'm not sure that team bonding is all that important. What's important is that a team works together well, and that will come or not over the course of a project. It's also important that individuals feel respected and that they feel that their ideas are respected. Team bonding is not, "Did you take your team to enough dinners? Did you go out to the movies? Did you go to the circus?" Most people, even very hard-working people, want to have a life, to be with their families. I think that's more important than going out to the circus.

If a team is going to bond, it will mostly bond through work. A typicalteam works at the client for 10 to 14 hours a day, plus a day over the weekend at the office. That's plenty of time for bonding. Also, on an out-of-town study, team members will eat dinner together more often than not. Why, as a team leader, would you want to take up yet more of their time? If the team isn't bonding, how is a fancy dinner going to help? Will it make a bad work experience good? So, when managing your team, be selective with team-bonding activities. Try to get your team's "significant others" involved; this will help them understand what their loved ones— your teammates—are doing, and it will help you understand your teammates. Above all, respect your teammates' time. One former associate noted that, at McKinsey, the best team dinners were at lunch —they showed that the EM knew the associates had lives.

TAKE YOUR TEAM'S TEMPERATURE TO MAINTAIN MORALE Maintaining your team's morale is an on-going responsibility. If you don't do it, your team will not perform well. Make sure you know how your team feels.

CHAPTER SIX

MANAGING HIERARCHY

consulting way has something of a split personality when it comes to hierarchy. On the one hand, the Firm claims that it has no real hierarchy. On the other hand, any past or present can tell you that two hierarchies (at least) exist within consulting way. Both statements are correct.

AN AGGRESSIVE STRATEGY FOR MANAGING HIERARCHY If you have the stomach for it, assert your equality in the organization. Keep on doing it until someone tells you otherwise. Obviously, this is not a strategy for everyone.

Hierarchical management is a workplace leadership structure in which authority is assigned in ranks and employees take directions from their superiors. For example, in a human resources department, the human resources assistant -- who occupies the lowest rank -- provides administrative support for other H.R. employees as needed. The H.R. coordinator has authority over the assistant, and an H.R. generalist governs the H.R. coordinator. The H.R. generalist has superiors at the corporate level. Employees' roles and level of authority -- if any -- are clearly established.Leaders should exercise consideration, discretion and common sense. Give your employees some autonomy; tell them what you want them to do without dictating every step. People often prefer to handle their work using certain approaches; even if you disagree with an employee's methods, you may find that he is much more productive when given some freedom to do this. Always listen to your employees' concerns; they should know that they have a say in how the organization functions. After all, these individuals can provide valuable input through experience. If you need to criticize a subordinate, deliver it constructively and coach them, providing suggestions for improvement. Finally, never make decisions or give orders based on emotion. If you take your anger out on others, they will see you as arbitrary or inconsiderate.

CHAPTER SEVEN

DOING RESEARCH

The consulting way problem-solving process begins with research. Before a team can construct an initial hypothesis, before it can disaggregate a problem into its components and uncover the key drivers, it has to have information. At the start of a consulting career, most of his time is spent gathering data, whether from one of the Firm's libraries, from consulting many databases, or from the Internet. Gathering, filtering, and analyzing data is the skill exercised most by new associates. As a result,consultant learned a number of tricks for jump-starting their research. You can use these tricks to find the answers to your business problem too.

Whatever the problem, chances are that someone, somewhere, has worked on something similar. Maybe that person is in your organization and can answer all your questions in the course of a phone call. Maybe other people in your field, in another division or another company, have seen the same problem already—find out who they are and get to know them. Do your research and ask questions; you will save yourself a lot of time and effort. Your time is valuable, so don't waste it by reinventing the wheel!

McKinsey keeps an electronic database called PDNet* containing reports from recent engagements and internal research. When I was a first-year associate, one of my jobs at the start of an engagement was to search PDNet for anything that would shed light on our current project: comparable industries, comparable problems. Inevitably, any PDNet query produced a mountain of documents that I then had to wade through to find the few that might be relevant. Still, this long day's (and, as often as not, night's) work usually yielded something to point us in the right direction. McKinsey has other resources that help its consultants work smarter, not harder. These include an excellent business library that holds every business book or magazine you care to mention; it also has access to all the major commercial databases such as Lexis/Nexis, Dun & Bradstreet, Datastream, and the

Internet. Most important, the library has a dedicated staff of information specialists who work extremely hard to supply the consultants with information—whether from PDNet, the library, or any other source. The Firm also has a cadre of senior information specialists who are experts in particular industries; they were an especially valuable resource when we found ourselves working one month for a client in banking and the next for a jet engine manufacturer.

Start with the annual report. If you want to get up to speed on a company as quickly as possible, the first place to turn is the annual report. It's easy to obtain (many companies now post their annuals on the World Wide Web) and contains a great deal of information beyond the financial data. When you get a company's annual, turn first to the "Message to Shareholders" or "Chairman's Remarks" at the front. If you read the section carefully, and a little skeptically, you'll find out a lot about how the company has performed in the last year, where management hopes to take the company in the future, and the strategy for getting there. You'll usually also get a quick breakdown of key financial indicators such as stock price, revenue, and earnings per share. Go further into the annual, and you'll find out about the company's business units and product lines, who its senior managers are, and where the company has offices and production facilities. Then you can plough into the numbers. A company's annual report will get your research off to a rapid start. Look for outliers. When you've collected a large amount of data on a particular aspect of your problem, look for outliers— things that are especially good or bad. Use a computer to get a quick picture. For example, suppose you are collecting data on your company's sales force. Enter the average sales of each salesperson and divide it by the number of accounts served by that salesperson for, say, the last three years; this gives you the average sales per account. Type the data into your favorite spreadsheet software and sort the averages from lowest to highest. Then look at the two or three best and worst figures. Congratulations, you've just found a fruitful area for research. Figure out why the numbers are so good or bad and you'll be well on your way to fixing the problem. Look for best practice. There's an old saying that no matter how good you are at something, there's always somebody better. This is as true in business as it is anywhere else. Find out what the best performers in the industry are doing and imitate them. Often, this is the quickest antidote to poor performance. Usually, you can't find out about best practice in the library. You have to think creatively. If some of your competitors have best practice, they probably won't tell you their secrets. Talk to other people in the industry: suppliers, customers, Wall Street analysts, friends from business school, and so forth.

Sometimes you can find best practice within your company. Someone, some team, or some division is outperforming the rest of the company. Find out why. Figure out how to implement the top performer's secrets throughout your organization. The result will be a huge payoff to your business.

CHAPTER EIGHT

CONDUCTING INTERVIEWS

Interviewing is such an important part of the consulting problem-solving process that it merits its own chapter in this book, separate from research. You can learn a lot from reading magazine articles, books, and scholarly papers, but to get the nitty-gritty on an organization, you have to ask questions of and get answers from the people on the front line. Interviewing is a skill in its own right, and most people have no idea how to go about it. You might think that even though interviewing style is a good technique for consultants who need to get up to speed on unfamiliar industries, it is of little use to executives in more settled positions. I disagree. In today's business world, no matter who you are, from the most junior of junior managers to the most senior of senior vice presidents, you may find yourself in a situation where you need the information in someone else's head. You might be assigned to a multifunctional team as part of a merger; you might be told to set up and run a new business. The possibilities are endless, but they all require you to pick someone's brain, chew the fat, or get up to speed. Call it what you like, it's an interview when you ask questions and get answers. In this chapter, I will take you through the interviewing process, from preparing your interview guide to writing your thank-you note. If you read no other chapter of the book from start to finish, read this one. I think you'll learn something very valuable that you won't find elsewhere.

BE PREPARED: WRITE AN INTERVIEW GUIDE When you go into an interview, be prepared. You may have only 30 minutes with a person whom you may never see again. Know what you're going to ask.

"Write an interview guide." Many people resent being interviewed, or at least begrudge you the time that you are taking from their day. A guide is your best tool for getting what you want from interviewees and for making the best use of your time—and theirs. You must think on two levels when constructing your guide. First, and obviously, what are the questions to which you need answers? Write them all down in any order. Second, and more important, what do you really need from this interview? What are you trying to achieve? Why are you talking to this person? Defining your purpose will help you put your questions in the right order and phrase them correctly. It helps to know as much as possible about the interviewee in advance. Is she a prickly CEO who might bite your head off if you ask a sensitive question? Or is she a middle-level manager whose pleas for change in her organization have gone unheeded? Both might know the same piece of information, but you'd approach each one differently

we were taught that, as a rule, an interview should start with general questions and move on to specific ones. Don't dive right into a sensitive area like "What are your responsibilities?" or "How long have you been with the company?" Start with anodyne questions about, say, the industry overall.

This will help the interviewee "warm up" and allow you to develop rapport. When deciding on which questions to ask, you might want to include some to which you know the answer. This may sound counterintuitive, but it's really very useful. On questions of fact, asking a "ringer" will give you some insights into the interviewee's honesty and/ or knowledge. For complex issues, you may think you "know" the answer, but there may be more than one; you should find out as many as possible. Once you've written your guide, look at it and ask yourself, "What are the three things I most want to know by the end of the interview?" These are the things you will focus on when you go into the interviewee's office, the three things that you will try your hardest to obtain before you leave. Sometimes you won't even get those answers (see "Difficult Interviews" later in the chapter), and sometimes they'll come easily. Anything more is gravy. Finally, every interview guide should conclude with what I call the prototypical consulting way question. When you've asked all your questions, or you're running out of time, put away your guide and ask the interviewee if there's anything else he'd like to tell you or any question you forgot to ask. As often as not, the interviewee will say no, but every once in a while you'll strike paydirt. Remember that, chances are, the people you interview know their organizations, their business units, or their departments better than you do. They may know which problems are eluding senior managers, who's pushing which agenda, or where the bones are buried. And sometimes, if you're lucky, they'll tell you.

WHEN CONDUCTING INTERVIEWS, LISTEN AND GUIDE When you're picking people's brains, ask questions and then let them do the talking. Most people like to talk, especially if you let them know you're interested in what they're saying. Keep the interview on track by breaking in when necessary.

SEVEN TIPS FOR SUCCESSFUL INTERVIEWING Always think strategically when conducting an interview. You have a goal to reach and limited time to reach it. Here are seven tried-and-tested stratagems to help you get what you want from an interviewee. 1. Have the interviewee's boss set up the meeting. Going through the boss tells the interviewee that the interview is important. He'll be less likely to jerk you around if he knows his boss wants him to talk to you. 2. Interview in pairs. It's very difficult to conduct an effective interview on your own. You may be so busy taking notes that it becomes difficult to ask the right questions. You may miss nonverbal clues that the interviewee is giving. Sometimes, it is useful for a pair of interviewers to "tag-team"—switch roles from question poser to note taker during the session. The approach is especially effective when one of the interviewers has specific knowledge on certain issues that will be covered. Furthermore, it is always useful to have two different views of what actually happened in the interview. Just make sure that whoever writes up the interview notes corroborates them with the other interviewer. 3. Listen; don't lead. In most interviews, you are not looking for yes-or-no answers to your questions. You want exhaustive answers—as much information as possible. The way to get them is to listen. Talk as little as possible, just enough to keep the interview on track. Remember that the interviewee probably knows a lot more about her business than you do, and most of the information she gives you will be useful one way or another. Here's another trick for keeping the information flowing. Ask open-ended questions. If you ask yes-or-no or multiple-choice questions, that's all you will get. For example, suppose you want to find out when a store's busiest season is. You think it is either summer or winter, but you're not sure. If you ask the store manager, "Is your busiest season summer or winter?" she might say summer; she might say winter; or she might say, "Actually, it's spring," in which case, you've just highlighted your lack of knowledge about her business. If you ask her, "What is your busiest season?" she will give you the answer, and probably in more detail than if you gave her multiple choice—for example, "We're busiest in the spring, specifically at Easter." By asking the open-ended question, you get a much better result.

4. Paraphrase, paraphrase, paraphrase. Before going out on interviews, every consultant is trained to repeat back a subject's answers in slightly

different form. I cannot overstress how important this is. Most people do not think or speak in a completely structured way. They ramble, they digress, they jumble important facts among irrelevancies. If you repeat their own words back to them—ideally with some structure applied—then they can tell you whether you understood them correctly. Paraphrasing also gives the interviewee a chance to add information or amplify important points. 5. Use the indirect approach. An EM had on his team a new associate, fresh out of the Navy. The two had put together a very clear interview guide and had agreed on a specific set of goals for an interview with a middle-level manager at their client, so the EM let the associate take the lead. The associate proceeded to grill the manager aggressively in order to get precisely what he wanted, as if it were an interrogation rather than an interview. As you might imagine, the interviewee was rattled; he became defensive and essentially refused to cooperate. The moral of this tale is "Be sensitive to the interviewee's feelings." Understand that the person may feel threatened. Don't dive right into the tough questions. If you have to dance around the important issues for a few minutes, that's OK. Take time to make the interviewee comfortable with you and the interview process (for an in-depth discussion, see the next section). 6. Don't ask for too much. There are two reasons not to ask for everything the interviewee has. First, you might get it. When you write your interview guide, you narrow down your goals to the two or three most important questions. If you then ask the interviewee for the sum total of his knowledge of the widget industry, you may find yourself wading through a lot of information to get what you really need, if you even find it at all. Second, you want to stop short of the straw that breaks the camel's back. Remember, being interviewed, especially in the context of a business problem, is an uncomfortable experience for many. If you compound that discomfort by pressing too hard, you may find that the interviewee becomes uncooperative or even hostile. You never know when you may want to come back to this person for more information, so don't shut the door. 7. Adopt the Columbo tactic. If you watched TV in the 1970s, you may remember Peter Falk's trenchcoat wearing detective, Lieutenant Columbo. After he finished quizzing a murder suspect about her whereabouts on the night in question, he would pick up his rumpled raincoat and head out the door. As he reached the threshold and was about to leave, he would turn around, stick his finger up to his temple, and say, "Excuse me, ma'am, but there's something I forgot to ask." This question invariably gave Columbo the answer he needed to figure out who did it.

If there's a particular question you need the answer to, or a piece of data that you want, the Columbo tactic is often a good way to get it. Once the interview is over, everybody becomes more relaxed. The interviewee's sense that you have some power over him will have disappeared. He is far less likely to be defensive, and will often tell you what you need or give you the information you seek on the spot. Try it; it works. You might also want to try the "super-Columbo" tactic. Instead of turning around at the door, wait until a day or two has passed, then drop by the interviewee's office. You were just passing by and remembered a question you forgot to ask. Again, this makes you much less threatening, and makes it more likely that you will get the information you need.

DON'T LEAVE THE INTERVIEWEE NAKED Remember that, for many people, being interviewed about problems in their job or business can be unnerving. You have a responsibility to be sensitive to their fears. It's not only the right thing to do; it makes good business sense too.

DIFFICULT INTERVIEWS Conduct enough interviews and you will encounter difficult ones. Some of them are easy enough to handle, once you know how. Others will test your strength and spirit.

ALWAYS WRITE A THANK-YOU NOTE When you get back to your office after interviewing someone, take the time to write a thank-you letter. It's polite and professional, and could pay you back in unexpected ways.

BRAINSTORMING

When the study has been sold, the team assembled, and the preliminary research done, the real work can begin. Brainstorming is the sine qua non of strategic consulting. It's what the clients really buy. Let's face it. Most large, modern corporations are chock full of intelligent, knowledgeable managers who are darned good at day-to-day problem solving. the consulting way offers a new mindset, an outsider's view that is not locked into "the company way" of doing things. That's what clients need when problems cannot be solved within the organization, and it starts in a meeting room with a table, some chairs, a bunch of pads, pens and pencils, some markers, and a clean "white board."

Before the first brainstorming session, consultants do their homework. Everyone on the team reads the results of the PDNet and library searches. The associates put together and distribute "fact packs" based on their preliminary research. The ED, the EM, and possibly the more senior associates on the team come up with initial hypotheses that the team will then test to destruction. Brainstorming takes time. Typically, a consulting team blocks out two hours, if not more, for a brainstorming session. Some team leaders prefer weekends for their meetings, though this is not always looked on favorably by the other members of the team. These sessions often run well into the night, fueled by deliveries of pizza, Chinese food, or sushi (my personal favorite). I even recall some teams bringing in a six-pack or two of beer for a weekend session (presumably to stimulate the flow of ideas). consulting U.S. offices keep "menu books" of the favored local food delivery services; these books see a lot of use .The most important ingredient for successful brainstorming is a clean slate. There's no point calling a meeting if you're just going to look at the data in the same old way. You have to leave your preconceptions and prejudices at the door of the meeting room. That way, you are free to manipulate the facts in your mind.

I like to think of brainstorming as playing with that old puzzle Rubik's Cube. Each fact is a face on one of the small cubes. Turn the faces this way and that, and you'll come up with the answer, or at least an answer.

Another metaphor I like to use is shuffling a pack of cards. Each fact is a card. When you first open the pack, all the cards are in order. How boring. Shuffle the cards, or throw them into the air and see how they land. Now you might find some interesting patterns: straights, flushes, full houses. The same thing happens when you toss around facts and ideas.

PROPER PRIOR PREPARATION Although brainstorming has an airy-fairy, college bull session connotation to some, in reality effective brainstorming requires some hard-nosed advance work. The cardinal rule of brainstorming is that you cannot do it successfully in a vacuum. Before you go into that meeting, you have to know something about the problem you'll be working on. Don't just stride into the meeting expecting to wow everyone with your brilliance. As with all things McKinsey, there is a method to preparing for your brainstorming session, whether you are the leader (or, as some prefer, moderator or facilitator) or just a participant. If you have followed the outline of Part Two sequentially—that is, you've completed your research—then half your preparation is done already. Now make sure that everyone on the team knows what you know. Put your research into what The consulting way call a "fact pack," a neatly organized summary of the key points and data that you've discovered, and circulate it to your team. If you are the leader, make sure that all your team members put their research into fact packs. Making a fact pack is easy. It doesn't require a detailed structure, just a little thought about what is important and how to show it. Once everyone on the team has read all the fact packs, you'll all have the same knowledge base when it comes time to generate ideas. Once you have absorbed your team's fact base, what next? McKinsey-ites fall into two camps on this subject. The first group says, "Familiarize yourself with the outlines of the problem and the data. Don't try to come up with an answer before the session starts." The counterproposition states, "Always come in with a hypothesis; otherwise, you waste too much time flailing around looking for ideas." I come down firmly between these two assertions—they're both right. If you can come up with a hypothesis, fine; if you're the team leader, you probably ought to have one. Just don't march into the team room saying, "This is the answer." The right attitude is, "I think this may be how things are. Let's attack this hypothesis as a group."IN A WHITE ROOM The point of brainstorming is the generation of new ideas.

So start with tabula rasa—a clean slate. When you get your team into the room, leave your preconceptions at the door. Bring the facts you know, but find new ways of looking at them.

Again, brainstorming is about generating new ideas. If all the team members come into the room saying the same old things and agreeing with one another, then you've gained nothing and wasted time. Even worse, if the team leader comes in and imposes her view on everyone else, the team has missed an opportunity to achieve a solution that's more creative and, possibly, better. Brainstorming requires the participation of everyone in the room, from the most senior director to the most junior analyst— and there's no guarantee on any given day that the former will have better ideas than the latter. No one should be afraid to speak his mind in the brainstorming room. So, along with your preconceptions, check your hierarchy and deference at the door. Here's an example of how not to run a brainstorming session. When Kristin Asleson was a new associate, the SEM on her engagement called the team members in for a brainstorming session. When they got there, the SEM said, "Just be quiet and watch me work through the problem on the white board." They then sat there for the next hour watching the SEM think to himself. It may have been instructive, but it wasn't brainstorming, unless it was brainstorming as theater. Here are a few more "rules of the road" for successful brainstorming. There are no bad ideas. No one should ever hesitate to open her mouth during a brainstorming session for fear of getting zinged with the words "That's a bad idea." If the idea was sincerely meant, but you disagree with it, take a minute to explain why. Debating ideas is part of the brainstorming process. Who knows? After a few minutes of discussion it, it might not seem such a bad idea after all. At least give it a chance. Obviously, ideas that are not directed at the problem at hand don't count—for example, "Let's forget about the problem and go play Frisbee" (unless you think the team might benefit from a quick game). There are no dumb questions. Just as there are no bad ideas, any question should be taken on its merits. Never be afraid to ask why something is the way it is or is done the way it's done. Often the answer is "Well, gee, that's the way we've always done it"— which is not a good reason to do much of anything. Never discount the benefits of working through seemingly obvious or simple questions. For example, when I was working on an engagement for a money management company, at our first brainstorming meeting, the brand-new associate on our team asked, "How much money is there in the world?" Rather than just saying "lots," we spent the next 45 minutes thinking through the dynamics of international money management and came out with some useful insights. Be prepared to kill your babies. This rather shocking notion originated among Hollywood screenwriters. It means that if your idea, no matter how good, is not part of the team's answer at the end of the session, dispense with it. Look upon your hypothesis as just one more datum to throw into the brainstorming mix. Offer it up to your teammates and let them knock it around. It may be "right" or it may be "wrong," but the main thing is that it should help the team think through the problem at hand. Don't invest a lot of your ego in your hypothesis; don't come to the meeting prepared to die in a ditch defending it. Know when to say when. Brainstorming takes time, but if you stay at it too long, you'll hit the point of rapidly diminishing returns. The consensus among former the consulting way that a team can stand about two hours of brainstorming before the atmosphere deteriorates. In my opinion, this time frame is especially true of evening sessions. Unless the team is composed completely of night .

owls, people become tired, cranky, and slow off the mark as the night wears on. There are always exceptions, of course. Sometimes you get on a roll and the adrenaline keeps you productive until well past midnight. Sometimes you gain insight by contemplating your colleague's plate of leftover fried rice.

If you must hold an all-day session, you have to make sations go on tangents; allow people to make jokes and let off steam, but rein them in after a little while to keep them focused. Take breaks every now and then—and not just for lunch, dinner, and calls of nature. If you can take a half-hour walk somewhere, do so. It's a great opportunity for people to gather their thoughts and stretch their legs.

The key to successful brainstorming is good preparation and a proper frame of mind. Here are a few tricks that consultants use to get the maximum benefit from their brainstorming sessions.

The Post-itTM exercise. Give everyone in the room a pad of sticky notes. The participants then write out any relevant ideas they have, one idea per note, and hand them over to the leader, who reads them aloud. This is a very good way to generate a lot of ideas quickly without getting bogged down in discussing each one as it comes out.

The flipchart exercise. Put a number of flipcharts around the room, each one labeled with a different category or issue. Each team member then goes around the room writing ideas down on the appropriate flipchart. If you like, you can give each team member a different colored marker, so you know whose ideas are whose.

We invited all the relevant players into a large room to discuss options for change at the client. We asked them to tell us up front everything they didn't like about the program we had presented. Once they had vented, we asked them to come up with things that were good about it, and ways that it could be implemented within their own business units— this required some "tough love" from our ED. The technique worked in two ways: It yielded some excellent ideas that we would not have otherwise come up with; and it helped a previously skeptical, if not outright hostile, management team buy into consulting way solution.

One more tip for handling a grumbler or rabble-rouser at a brainstorming session: Have the leader or moderator stand behind him, and even touch him on the shoulder occasionally. This lets the troublemaker know that he is being watched. If he mutters an aside, the moderator can ask him to speak up, rather like the teacher who tells the note-passing student, "Why don't you share it with the class?" Try these exercises to jazz up your own brainstorming sessions. You'll be impressed with the results.

CHAPTER TEN

MAKING PRESENTATIONS

Consultants communicates with its clients through presentations. They may be formal presentations: meetings held around boardroom tables with neatly bound blue books. They may be informal presentations between a few managers at the client and a couple of consultants with several charts hastily stapled together into a deck. As junior members advance through the ranks at the Firm, they spend a lot of time presenting ideas to other people. consulting way has become extremely good at communicating in this way. You can apply many of the Firm's techniques in your own presentations. They will help you get your message across—which, after all, is the goal of the process.

For your presentation to succeed, it must take the audience down the path of your logic in clear, easy to follow steps.

A presentation reflects the thinking of the person or team that put it together. If your presentation is sloppy and muddled, your audience will assume that your thinking is also sloppy and muddled—regardless of whether that is the case. So, whatever structure you applied to your thought process, apply it to your presentation. If you use the consutants structure, use it in your presentation. If you prefer some other organizing principle, make sure your presentation reflects it—assuming, of course, that your thought process is structured and logical.

Let me reiterate that you do not have to use the The consulting way structure if you are not comfortable with it—if it is not the way you think. A friend of mine at business school became an entrepreneur; like many entrepreneurs, he was capable of brilliant insights and intuitive leaps, but his thinking was not particularly organized. He made many successful presentations using the basic structure of "Tell 'em what you're going to tell 'em, tell 'em, tell 'em what you told 'em." He followed a structure and it worked for him.

Usually, if you adhere to a structure that makes a step-by-step progression, you want the audience to follow your presentation at your pace. There's usually someone in the audience who lacks the patience for this. One consulting way EM faced the problem of a senior manager at his client who, when handed a presentation document, would invariably leaf through it from beginning to end and then "tune out" for the rest of the meeting. But the EM found a solution. For his team's final presentation, he handed the manager a blue book with all the pages stapled together—no more leafing.

REMEMBER THAT THERE ARE DIMINISHING MARGINAL RETURNS TO EFFORT Resist the temptation to tweak your presentation right up to the last minute. Weigh the value of a change against a good night's sleep for you and your team. Don't let the best be the enemy of the good.

THE CONSULTING WAY bound together by a set of common experiences: training programs, interviews, "all-nighters," and more. One of the most common and most unnecessary experiences shared by almost every associate in the Firm is the 4 a.m. vigil in the copier room waiting for the presentation booklets to be put together for tomorrow's (although now it's today's) big progress review. I once spent a pleasant two hours early one morning removing one chart from 40 spiral-bound copies of a blue book and replacing it with a new version, all because of one typo. Another associate and his EM worked through the night cutting and pasting new numbers onto a chart with razor blades and a glue stick (this was before computer graphics became widely available at the Firm). Many businesspeople and many organizations will accept nothing less than perfection. In many cases, this is laudable: No one wants to ride in an airplane where the engine mounting bolts fit almost correctly. However, when you are preparing a presentation, even to the hardest-nosed CEO of the most powerful corporation, don't let the best be the enemy of the good. At some point, usually well before the actual presentation, nitpicking changes no longer add value. Learn to recognize that point and draw the line on changes well in advance of the meeting. Think about it this way: What matters more, that your team gets a good night's sleep before the presentation or that there is a typo in the final document? Every document of any length will have a few typos, no matter how hard you search and despite spellchecking software (or, sometimes, because of it). On rare occasions, that typo may have to be corrected, but only rarely. Far better that you come to the presentation rested, not harried and bedraggled; giving a presentation is stressful enough as it is. Drawing the line on changes requires discipline. If yours is the final say on the presentation, you just have to discipline yourself. Tell yourself and your team that you want the documents printed, copied, bound, or transferred onto slides—whatever it is that you need—at least 24 hours before the big moment. Spend the time between then and the presentation rehearsing, discussing possible questions that may arise, or just taking a relaxed day at the office, if you can.

PREWIRE EVERYTHING A good business presentation should contain nothing new for the audience. Walk all the players at the client through your findings before you gather them into one room.

Imagine it is the start of your final presentation. Your findings have been kept confidential to avoid any leaks into the market. You and your team are meeting with the top executives of your company, who are eager finally to hear your recommendations. Your boss is here; your boss's boss is here; the heads of all your company's business units are here; your CEO is sitting at the head of the table hanging on your every word. You begin to speak. "Ladies and gentlemen," you say, "after weeks of exhaustive research, my team and I have reached the conclusion that the future of our company requires us to increase our investment in widget production by 75 percent over the next two years." As you reach for your first chart of backup analysis, a murmur is heard from the audience. The director of the gadgets division is incensed. Surely, he says, the future of the company lies with gadgets. The CFO protests that the company doesn't have that level of funds available. The president of the widgets subsidiary rushes to your defense. Your moment in the corporate sun dissolves into a shouting match. Clearly, not everyone likes surprises.

To avoid this disaster scenario, consultants engage in "prewiring." Before they hold a presentation or progress review, a team will take all the relevant players in the client organization through their findings in private. That way, there are few, if any, surprises on the big day. As one former EM said, "It was very rare for us to do a presentation where we hadn't taken the various players through our findings beforehand. Otherwise, it was just too risky. In effect, the actual presentation became performance art." When prewiring, you must remember the cardinal rule of being a successful consultant or corporate troubleshooter: Not only do you have to come up with the "right" answer; you also have to sell that answer to your client. Sometimes, this just requires salesmanship; other times, it takes compromise. Suppose you walk into the office of Bob, the Director of the

Gadgets Division, and tell him that you think the answer is to invest more in widgets, at the expense of gadgets. He is unlikely to be pleased, but when you are alone with him in his office, you are far more likely to be able to take him through your analysis step by step. By the end of the process, the gadgets director may be convinced (great, move on to the next person) or he may come up with some fact you hadn't known about that alters your recommendation (which does happen, believe me), or he may refuse to accept your recommendation without some changes. In the last case, you have to negotiate. If the compromise is small, make it and move on; if his demands are too great, you will have to figure out a way to bypass him. Of course, if he throws you out of his office (unlikely, but possible), you have a problem on your hands the size of which is in proportion to the director of gadgets' power in the organization. Let's go back to our scenario at the beginning of this section. This time, though, imagine that you have prewired your presentation with all the senior managers at the table, including the unrelenting director of gadgets. "Ladies and gentlemen," you say, "after weeks of exhaustive research, my team and I have reached the conclusion that the future of our company requires us to increase our investment in widget production by 75 percent over the next two years." As you reach for your first slide, the direc110 Selling Solutions tor of gadgets says, "I've heard this before, and it's horse ———. We have to increase our gadget production." The CFO raises an eyebrow, but says nothing—you've already shown him how he can fund the additional investment. The SVP of the widget subsidiary, secure in the knowledge that she will be the winner at the end of today's presentation, merely looks in the direction of the CEO. The CEO leans back in his chair, steeples his fingers, and tells the gadgets director: "Now come on, Bob, I think we're all pulling on the same oar here. Let's get through the presentation, then we can discuss it at the end." You already know what that outcome will be. Isn't it better to skip the surprise ending?

CHAPTER ELEVEN

DISPLAYING DATA WITH CHARTS

CONSULTANTS relies on charts, graphical representations of information, as a primary means of communicating with its cover what works with charts and what does not. You can find most of this wisdom in a book by Gene Zelazny, the Firm's guru of charts and presentations, entitled Say It With Charts.* It's an excellent resource and I don't intend to repeat its contents here. In this chapter, I explain the overarching CONSULTING WAY philosophy of charts, and why it will work for you. I also share with you the one McKinsey chart that I have never seen used outside the Firm. clients. The Firm has devoted a lot of time and effort .

KEEP IT SIMPLE — ONE MESSAGE PER CHART The more complex a chart becomes, the less effective it is at conveying information. Use charts as a means of getting your message across, not as an art project.

The information in a chart may be highly complex and expressive of multiple points or ideas; the job of the chartist is to pick which point to make. consultants do this with the "lead," the caption at the top of the chart. A good lead expresses the point of the chart in one simple sentence. The salient information in the chart may be highlighted, with a different shading, an exploded pie slice, or (as I've done here) with an arrow, among other methods. If a chart offers several insights, copy it with a new lead and the relevant information highlighted.

USE A WATERFALL CHART TO SHOW THE FLOW The waterfall chart—seldom seen outside McKinsey and not generally available in computer graphics packages—is an excellent way to illustrate quantitative flows.

When you looked at each sample chart in the last section, you probably wondered exactly what type of chart you were seeing. It looked something like a column chart, but not like any you'd find in the chart libraries of Excel™, Freelance™, or any of the other popular computer graphics packages. The chart may have looked strange, but I'll bet you didn't have a lot of trouble understanding it. It's called a waterfall chart, and CONSULTANTS use it all the time, although it's rarely found anywhere else.

The waterfall chart is an excellent method of illustrating how you get from number A to number B. The charts in Figures 11-1 and 11-2 depict a simplified income statement, starting with sales on the left and ending with net income on the right, and show the various items that lead from one to the other. The starting point (sales in the example) is always a column that begins at zero. Positive items such as interest income are depicted as columns that start at the high point of the preceding column and reach upward. Negative items such as operating expenses are columns that start at the high point of the preceding column and extend downward. The total is the distance from the top of the last item (or bottom if that item is negative) to the zero line. Subtotals can be included along the way in the same manner. Waterfalls can depict static data (balance sheets, income statements) or active data (time series data, cashflows). You can mix negative and positive items (e.g., we started with 6 accounts, gained 3 in the first quarter, then lost 2 in the next quarter, for a total of 7), or you can segregate them to show, say, where value is created and where it is destroyed (e.g., we make money in widgets, gadgets, and thingamajigs; we lose money in flummeries, frankincense, and myrrh). Whatever data you use, the waterfall chart is a versatile way to convey a lot of information in a clear, concise manner. So go with the flow.

CHAPTER TWELVE

MANAGING INTERNAL COMMUNICATIONS

The success of a team-based operation depends on open communication, both from the top down and from the bottom up. Consultants has the same methods of internal communication as those available to any modern organization: voice mail, e-mail, memos, meetings, the water fountain, and so forth. It is fair to say that in the area of internal communications the Firm as a whole has no new insights to offer. On the other hand, former consultants, in their many combined years of experience, have garnered a number of useful methods for managing internal communications that you can use.

I've mentioned the famous Mushroom Method of management: "Keep them in the dark, cover them with manure, and see what crops up." Most people don't realize that the Mushroom Method can operate in both directions; it is possible to keep your boss in the dark too. No matter which direction the manure is dumped, the Mushroom Method is unproductive. For a successful team operation, you have to keep the information flowing. Make sure your team is up to date with at least the broad outlines of your project. This is especially true of large undertakings. Being "in the loop" will help your teammates understand how their work is contributing to the final goal, how their efforts are worthwhile. Conversely, when people feel that they are working in a vacuum, that they are alienated from the greater enterprise, their morale is sure to suffer. Also, if you keep your teammates up to date, they'll return the favor. At the ground level, they may be closer to events than you are. Good information flow can help you spot emerging problems (or opportunities) faster. Always keep your boss up to date with your team's progress. Don't think that your boss will stay out of your way if you keep her in the dark. She'll be far more comfortable when she knows that everything is under control. If things are not under control, then you want your boss to know exactly what the problems are so she can apply her expertise as effectively as possible.

There are two basic methods of internal communication: the 120 Selling Solutions message (whether in the form of voice mail, e-mail, or memo) and the meeting. I'll suggest some tips for successful messages in the next section. Right now, let's concentrate on meetings. Meetings form the glue that holds your team together. Team meetings allow excellent information flow, in all directions, and provide a certain amount of social bonding. They help remind those present that they are part of a team. Suzanne Tosini, a former McKinsey EM and now a senior manager at Freddie Mac, noted that one of the keys to a successful meeting is making sure everyone attends. To ensure that people do show up, make team meetings a regular item on everybody's schedule. If you have nothing to discuss, then cancel the meeting (as far in advance as possible); your teammates can always find a use for the extra 45 minutes. Suzanne's other two keys for a successful meeting are an agenda and a leader. Keep the number of items on your agenda to the minimum needed to make sure everyone is up to date with important events, issues, and problems. If something can be put on hold for another time, it probably should. If you are the leader, make sure you cover your agenda as briskly as possible: Frequent meetings are good, unnecessarily long ones are not. One other method of internal communication is in a class by itself: learning by walking around. Some of the most valuable conversations in my experience resulted from random encounters—in the corridors, at the water cooler, on the way to lunch, at the Firm, or at the client. You can gain a lot just by wandering around and talking to people, and they can learn a lot from you. Never underestimate the value of the random fact. However you choose to communicate with your team, make sure that you do so frequently and openly. You will boost your team's efficiency and morale, as well as your boss's peace of mind. Turn on the lights and clear out the manure!

THE THREE KEYS TO AN EFFECTIVE MESSAGE A good business message has three attributes: brevity, thoroughness and structure. Include all three in every voice mail, e-mail or memo you send and you'll get your message across.

A message, whether it's an e-mail, a voice mail, a memo, or a sticky note covered in cramped handwriting, is a presentation in miniature—a means of conveying information to an audience. As such, an effective message shares the same properties as an effective presentation: It is brief, covering only the points the audience needs to know; it is thorough, covering all the points the audience needs to know; and it has a structure that conveys those points clearly to its audience. 1. Brevity. Brevity, or rather the lack of it, is much more of a problem in spoken than written communications. Many businesspeople can write concise memos, but how many can record a concise voice mail? To join that select group, think before you speak (or write). Whittle down your message to the three or four points that the audience needs to know. If necessary, write these things down on paper. Some consultants write the entire message out like a script before sending a voice mail to their ED or DCS. I think that's going a bit too far—just the bullet points will do. 2. Thoroughness. Make sure your message contains everything your audience needs to know. You are not trying to keep your audience in suspense. Don't just tell your boss, "I'm doing X, Y, and Z. Call me if you have any questions." Tell her not only what you are doing, but what the issues are and what your thoughts are on them. Don't just check in; it's a waste of your boss's time (and yours). If you don't have anything useful to say, wait until you do.

3. Structure. To be readily understood, a message must follow a structure, and that structure must be readily apparent to the audience. Even if you're just writing a one-page e-mail or leaving a 30-second voice message, a simple structure will help your message get through. It can be as basic as this: We have three problems. In order of increasing importance, they are: 1. Our widgets are too expensive. 2. Our sales force is incompetent. 3. Our widget factory was just destroyed in a freak meteorite impact. Sometimes McKinsey-ites can take structuring their messages a bit too far. One EM in the New York office was reputed to put her shopping lists in Firm format. Another left affectionate messages on his wife's answering machine—following the McKinsey structure. Although you needn't follow the extreme examples of these overzealous consultants in your business communications you would do well to remember the three keys to effective messaging.

ALWAYS LOOK OVER YOUR SHOULDER You cannot be an effective consultant if you don't maintain confidentiality. Know when you can talk and when you can't. Be just a bit paranoid.

CHAPTER THIRTEEN

WORKING WITH CLIENTS

It goes without saying that without clients there would be no consulting way. They pay the (enormous) bills that keep the Firm going. It is not, therefore, surprising that McKinsey-ites are always told to put the client first. Hamish McDermott remarked that there was one true hierarchy at consulting: client, firm, you (in descending order). In this chapter, we will cover the two different aspects of working with clients the consulting way. We will start with techniques to get the most out of a client team, the people from the client organization who work with consulting way to reach a solution; we'll also look at ways to keep a client team from doing more harm than good. We will then move on to managing the client—in case, the senior people at the client organization who had called in the Firm to begin with. You will learn how to keep your clients engaged and supportive of your efforts and also how to make sure your solution actually gets implemented rather than gathering dust on a high shelf.

For some readers, the issue of client teams may seem remote. After all, if you are not a consultant, when will you actually have to deal with client teams? The answer is sooner than you might think. As a problem solver in a large organization, you may find yourself working with a team from, say, another business unit. Or you may be working on a joint venture with a team from an entirely different organization. In that case, you will, I hope, find the discussion of client teams as useful as the discussion of managing your client.

When you're working with a client team, you and the team have to work together or you won't work at all. Make sure that members of the client team understand why their efforts are important to you and beneficial for them.

HOW TO DEAL WITH "LIABILITY" CLIENT TEAM MEMBERS You may find that not everyone on the client team has the same abilities or goals as you do. Get "liability" members off the client team if you can; otherwise, work around them. There are two kinds of "liability" members on a client team: the merely useless and the actively hostile. Ideally, neither type is on your team. If your career is typical, you'll probably get both.

On an engagement for a large New York bank, my team worked with a client team staffed with senior managers from various departments within the client organization: lending, investing, back office, and so on. Our member from the back office was a man I'll call Hank. Hank was, shall we say, a diamond in the rough. He stood 6'4" tall and looked like a former football player who had let himself go—which, in fact, he was. His ties never matched his shirts and he invariably had food stains on his suit coat. Also, Hank knew his area of the bank inside and out and was probably as smart as any member of the consulting team. Hank didn't want to work with consulting. He thought that the Firm peddled an expensive line of baloney to credulous clients and left the employees to clean up afterward He didn't want to be on the client team—he had real work to do. Still, his boss had assigned him to the team, so he showed up every day, and stubbornly refused to contribute. In short, Hank was useless. How do you handle a Hank, or someone who is just too dumb or incompetent to do the work required of him? As a first (and easiest) tactic, you can try to trade the liability out of your team and get somebody better. Trading doesn't always work, however; there might be no one better available and you're stuck with your own Hank. In that case, you have to deal with Hank. Work around him. Give him a discrete section of the work that he can do; make sure it is neither critical to the project nor impossible for anyone else on the team to do. You'll have to rely on the other members of the team pick up the slack. For all his faults, Hank was better than Carlos. A superslick operator (BA, Oxford; MBA, Harvard) from Argentina, Carlos was the leader of the client team and our main liaison with the most senior management at the client. He was also a saboteur. Carlos had the patronage of a board-level faction within the client company that did not want consulting there; these board members felt they knew which direction consulting would recommend and they didn't like it.

ENGAGE THE CLIENT IN THE PROCESS If the client doesn't support you, your project will stall. Keep your clients engaged by keeping them involved. To succeed as a management consultant or a business troubleshooter you must keep your client—be it your boss or the management of an organization that has hired you from the outside—engaged in the problem-solving process. Being engaged in the process means supporting your efforts, providing resources as needed, and caring about the outcome. With engagement thus defined, it is hard to imagine how any project could succeed without an engaged client. The first step in keeping your clients engaged is to understand their agenda. Clients will support you only if they think your efforts contribute to their interests. Remember that their interests may change over time. Frequent contact and regular updates— even if it's just by memo—will help you keep in touch with your clients and keep your projects "top of mind" for them. Get on a client's calendar up front. Schedule progress meetings with tentative topics; if you need to reschedule, do it later.

They give your clients something to sink their teeth into and make them feel included in the problem-solving process. The long-run returns on your work will be much greater if your clients feel that they were involved in reaching the solution and that they understood it, rather than being handed the solution neatly wrapped and tied with pink ribbon. This brings us to one of the ironies of consulting.

GET BUY-IN THROUGHOUT THE ORGANIZATION If your solution is to have a lasting impact on your client, you have to get support for it at all levels of the organization. If you come up with a brilliant solution, structure it logically, and present it to your client with clarity and precision, then your job is done and you can go home, right? Wrong! If you want to create real change that has lasting impact, you must get acceptance for your solution from everyone in the organization that it affects. For instance, suppose you tell your board of directors that they can boost widget profitability by reorganizing the widget sales force and streamlining the widget production process. Your argument is compelling; the board ratifies your suggestion; champagne corks pop and cigars ignite. One slight hitch remains: What do the sales force and the production-line workers think about all this? If they don't like your ideas, if they put up a fight, then your solution will not be implemented. It will end up on the great remainder shelf of business, right next to the Betamax. To avoid this dire fate, you must sell your solution to every level of the organization, from the board on down. After you've presented to the board, present to middle-level managers. They will probably have day-to-day responsibility for implementing, so let them know what's going on. Don't neglect the people on the line, either. The changes you recommend may have the greatest effect on them, so their buy-in is vital to a successful implementation. Finally, serial presentations give the junior members of your team a good opportunity to hone their presentation skills. Tailor your approach to your audience. Don't make the same presentation to, say, the fleet drivers as you would to the CEO. At the same time, respect your audience. Explain what is being done and why. Show people the entire picture. Let them know how their jobs fit into the organization as a whole. They're not stupid; they'll understand. Treat them with respect (remember, a lot of the time they don't get any) and they will respond positively most of the time.

BE RIGOROUS ABOUT IMPLEMENTATION Making change happen takes a lot of work. Be rigorous and thorough. Make sure someone takes responsibility for getting the job done. Implementing recommendations for change is a big subject. Whole books can be (and have been) written on it. I will limit myself here to explaining a few ground rules that McKinsey consultants have learned for implementing change. To implement major change, you must operate according to a plan. Your implementation plan should be specific about what will happen and when—at the lowest possible level of detail. Don't just write: We must reorganize the widget sales force. Instead, write: We must reorganize the widget sales force. • Hold training sessions for all sales regions Reallocate sales staff to new sales teams by customer type. Take new sales teams to call on top 20 customers. (Start: April 1. Responsibility: Harriet.) One former EM gave a no-holds-barred recipe for a successful implementation plan: State what needs to be done, and when it needs to be done by, at such a level of detail and clarity that a fool can understand it.

Enough said. Make specific people responsible for implementing the solution. Be careful about whom you pick. Make sure people have the skills necessary to get the job done. Enforce your deadlines and don't allow exceptions unless absolutely necessary. The right point person can make implementation a very smooth process. If that person is not going to be you, make sure you pick someone who can "kick butt and take names." At one McKinsey client, an international bank, the managers chose a rather frightening fellow named Lothar to implement a major change program in their back-office processing. Lothar, who looked and sounded a bit like Arnold Schwarzenegger, had a very simple technique for getting the job done. Using the detailed consulting implementation plan, he assigned specific tasks to members of his team. Every two weeks the team would meet, and anybody who had not accomplished his or her tasks for the period had to explain the failure to the entire group. After the first meeting, when a few of the team members had undergone a grilling from Lothar, no one ever missed a deadline.

CHAPTER FOURTEEN

ASSISTANT IS A LIFELINE

Call the position secretary, administrative assistant, or whatever. The person who takes your messages; keeps your schedule; does your typing, duplicating, and filing; and performs a dozen other office tasks is an exceptionally valuable resource. Treat your secretary well.

To attract the best, the Firm provides a real career path for secretaries. New recruits usually start out working with four or five associates. The good ones move on to work for SEMs; the best get claimed by partners and directors. Secretaries receive regular training, just like consultants, and they even get their own "retreat" every year. But there's more to the path than that. Many of the managers running the Firm's administrative and recruiting functions started out as secretaries; now they have positions of considerable power and responsibility. All this is designed to help consultant way attract and retain the best secretaries, just as it seeks to attract and retain the best consultants.

A good secretary will perform numerous tasks that make a consultant's life easier. These range from the obvious, such as typing, filing, and duplicating, to the not-so-obvious: filling out time sheets, paying credit card bills for consultants on long assignments, and sending flowers to significant others after yet another missed date. In fact, it is the less obvious tasks that really make a difference in a consultant's life. Most consultant can do their own typing, many handle their own filing, and anyone can run the copier in a pinch. But knowing that there is someone "back home" whom you can trust to do those other, niggling little things that you would normally do if you were not 500 miles from your apartment for the next six months—that's going to make your life easier! The alternative is pretty ugly. I saw a number of associates whose lives were a living hell because their secretaries were not up to scratch. Files got lost; faxes misdirected; messages appeared days after they were taken; clients were upset by poor telephone manners.

www.ingramcontent.com/pod-product-compliance
Lightning Source LLC
Chambersburg PA
CBHW030811170726
47995CB00011B/458